Everything you want to know about
Dinosaurs

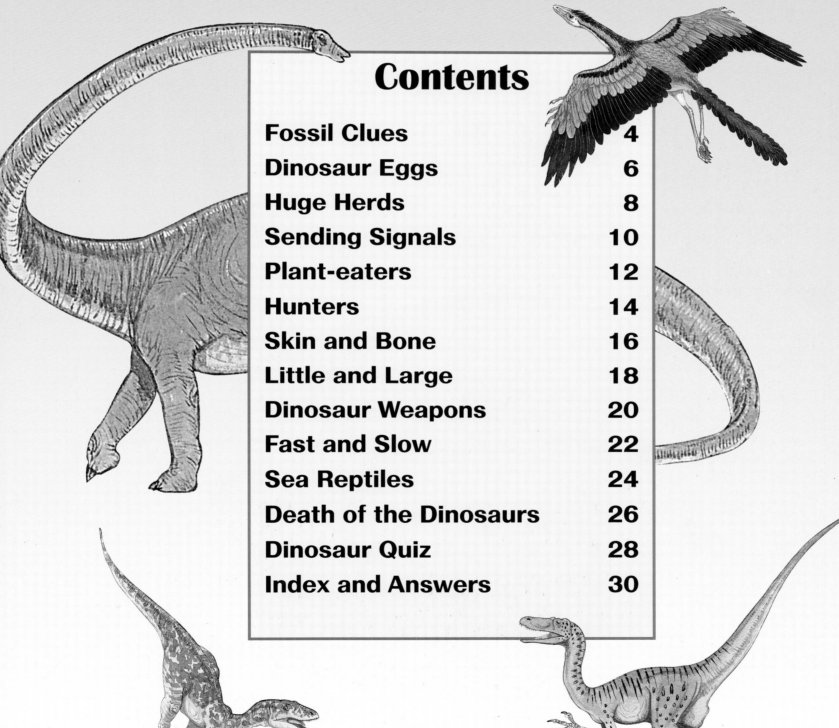

Contents

T S

Fossil Clues

Dinosaurs lived on Earth millions of years ago, long before people existed. We only know about them from the clues they left behind. When a dinosaur died, the soft parts of its body soon rotted away. The hard parts, such as bones, teeth, and claws, lasted longer. Some dinosaur remains have been preserved in rocks for millions of years. Over that time they have turned into stone. We call these stones fossils. Experts, called palaeontologists, dig up these fossils and use them to find out about dinosaurs. Palaeontologists can work out what a dinosaur looked like and how it lived.

What can fossil bones tell us?

Fossil bones can tell us a lot about an animal. Leg bones tell us its size and how it moved. Its teeth tell us what it ate. Skull bones, from the head, give clues about what it looked like and how it lived. This long narrow skull belonged to *Dromiceiomimus* (dro-miss-ee-oh-my-mus). Its large eye sockets and big braincase suggest that this dinosaur had good eyesight and was clever.

Have dinosaur teeth been found?

Yes, teeth are very hard and tough so they don't rot away easily. This means they often get preserved as fossils. Fossil teeth can give us lots of clues about an animal. The shape, size, and cutting edge of a tooth can tell us how a dinosaur lived and what it ate. *Heterodontosaurus* (het-er-oh-dont-oh-saw-rus) had teeth of different shapes. This means it probably ate lots of different foods. This was unusual for a dinosaur.

How are fossils formed?

1. When this dinosaur died in a flood, its body sank to the bottom of the riverbed. It lay there, in the mud, for many years.

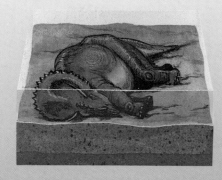

2. Slowly the soft parts of the dinosaur, such as the flesh, rotted away. The body became buried under layers of mud.

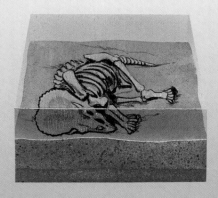

Did all dinosaurs have claws?

Yes, most dinosaurs had claws. Nails and claws are hard so they last well. Over time, some of them have turned into fossils. The size and shape of a dinosaur's claws are clues to the way the dinosaur lived. Long, sharp claws, like those of today's tigers, could be used to rip and tear food. One of the first dinosaurs, *Herrerasaurus* (herra-ra-saw-rus), had long finger claws. Perhaps it used them to grab small animals to eat.

What kinds of fossil have been found?

Most fossils are bones and teeth, but other types of fossil have been found as well. Fossil eggs, footprints, and bits of scaly skin have also been dug up. Sometimes even droppings became fossilized. Animal dung contains bits and pieces of food, so scientists can tell what food the dinosaur ate. Giant dinosaurs such as *Riojasaurus* (ree-ok-a-saw-rus) must have left huge mounds of dung. Luckily, fossil dung has turned to stone so it doesn't smell!

Did dinosaurs leave footprints?

Yes, when dinosaurs walked on soft mud or sand, they left deep footprints. Sometimes these became hard and turned into fossils. These footprints can give us clues to a dinosaur's size and weight. Some dinosaurs, such as *Camarasaurus* (kam-ar-a-saw-rus), left lots of tracks as they walked along together. This shows that they lived in groups, or herds.

3. Over millions of years the mud and bones turned into rock. The fossil dinosaur skeleton became buried beneath layers of rock.

4. Some fossils are revealed as the layers of rock are slowly worn away. Others are found when experts look for them and dig them up.

Dinosaur Eggs

Dinosaurs belonged to a group of animals called reptiles. Most living reptiles, such as crocodiles, turtles, snakes, and lizards, lay eggs which hatch into young. For a long time experts thought that dinosaurs probably laid eggs too, but no one knew for sure. Then, in 1922, a nest of fossil dinosaur eggs, laid millions of years before, was found. This proved that dinosaurs laid their eggs on land. Later, experts dug up nests containing fossils of newly hatched young, and eggs with babies still inside.

Where were dinosaur eggs first found?

The first dinosaur eggs were found in 1922, in the Gobi Desert in Mongolia. The eggs belonged to *Protoceratops* (pro-toh-serra-tops), a dinosaur that lived around 100 million years ago. The female *Protoceratops* scraped a nest hole in the ground for her eggs. As many as 30 eggs were found in one nest. The fossil eggs, each about the size of a tennis ball, were arranged in a neat spiral. Some experts think that two or more females laid their eggs in the same nest.

How big were dinosaur eggs?

Dinosaur eggs varied in size, depending on the size of the adults. But even the largest dinosaurs laid relatively small eggs. Some of the largest known dinosaur eggs, about 12 inches long, were laid by 40-foot-long *Hypselosaurus* (hip-sel-o-saw-rus). A female *Maiasaura* (my-a-saw-ra) was about 30 feet long—the size of a big bus. Each of her eggs was only 8 inches long—the size of a large ostrich egg. Groups of *Maiasaura* nested together. Their huge nesting sites covered whole hillsides.

Did dinosaurs build nests?

Many dinosaurs did build nests to lay their eggs in. In a herd of *Maiasaura*, all the females built their nests close together. This helped protect the nests from enemies.

1. First each female *Maiasaura* dug a big, deep hole. Then she laid her eggs in the hole. Experts believe she covered the eggs with lots of plants to keep them warm.

6

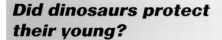

Did dinosaurs protect their young?

No one knows for sure, but some dinosaurs may have protected their young. An adult *Styracosaurus* (sty-rak-oh-saw-rus) was longer than two small cars. It was protected by long, sharp horns on its nose and neck frill. But, like all young animals, its babies were at risk from hungry meat-eaters. If attacked, the adult *Styracosaurus* may have formed a circle around their young, like musk oxen do today. The adults' horns would have pointed out toward the enemy, forming a spiny wall. The young stayed safely in the center.

Were dinosaur eggs eaten?

Eggs make a tasty meal for many animals. Dinosaur eggs were good food too, and dinosaurs probably ate each other's eggs. *Oviraptor* (ohv-ih-rap-tor) was a wolf-size dinosaur that could dart along at up to 30 miles an hour. It lived at the same time as *Protoceratops*. Perhaps it stole eggs from *Protoceratops'* nests. It may have cracked open the shells with its strong fingers.

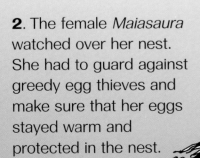

2. The female *Maiasaura* watched over her nest. She had to guard against greedy egg thieves and make sure that her eggs stayed warm and protected in the nest.

3. After several weeks the eggs began to crack and the baby *Maiasaura* hatched out. To begin with, the hatchlings were fed and cared for by their mother.

Huge Herds

There are lots of fossil clues to tell us how dinosaurs lived. Some clues suggest that many types of dinosaur lived in herds or packs. Huge tracks of fossil footprints, all going in the same direction, show that lots of dinosaurs walked along together. Experts think they were made by a herd of dinosaurs. Fossil nesting sites show that dinosaurs of the same kind often nested near one another. This means that the herd probably bred together, too. Huge numbers of dinosaur bones have been found buried in the same place. Experts believe these bones belonged to a herd that died together.

Why did dinosaurs live in herds?

Some small, plant-eating dinosaurs such as *Lesothosaurus* (lee-soo-too-saw-rus) probably lived in herds for safety. The more pairs of eyes on the lookout, the better chance the dinosaurs had of spotting danger, and warning the rest of the herd.

Did all dinosaurs live in herds?

A group of large meat-eaters could not hide easily. So, like tigers today, large carnivorous dinosaurs, such as *Indosuchus* (in-doh-soo-kus), probably hunted alone. Perhaps *Indosuchus* crept up on plant-eating dinosaurs, pouncing on one that had strayed from the herd.

Why did some herds die together?

Experts have suggested a story to explain how the remains of 40 *Allosaurus* (al-oh-saw-rus) ended up in a grave in Utah.
1. The *Allosaurus* were hunting near a swamp.

2. They spotted an *Apatosaurus* (a-pat-oh-saw-rus) bogged down in the mud. Thinking they had found an easy meal, the *Allosaurus* plunged into the swamp.

Did some dinosaurs hunt in packs?

Some small, meat-eating dinosaurs may have hunted in packs, just as wolves and hyenas do today. This would have allowed them to catch larger prey than if they hunted alone. A group of *Ornitholestes* (or-nith-oh-less-teez) would have been able to kill a large dinosaur by striking it from all sides. A wounded dinosaur would have found it hard to escape from so many attackers.

Why did some big dinosaurs live in herds?

Experts think some large, plant-eating dinosaurs lived in herds for protection. Hundreds of fossil bones of *Iguanodon* (ig-wa-no-don), each of which stood about 16 feet tall and weighed as much as an elephant, have been found jumbled together. Few predators would attack a group of huge animals.

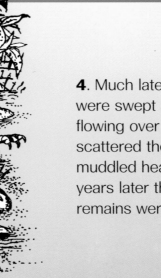

3. The *Allosaurus* were sucked down into the sticky mud, too. They struggled but could not get free. They all died in the boggy swamp.

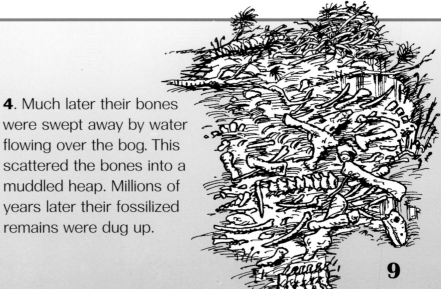

4. Much later their bones were swept away by water flowing over the bog. This scattered the bones into a muddled heap. Millions of years later their fossilized remains were dug up.

9

Sending Signals

Dinosaurs could not talk to one another the way we do, so they communicated in other ways. They probably used sounds, smells, touch, and visual signals, just as animals do today. Herds of animals often flash signals to each other. A sudden flash of color could be a warning of danger. Dinosaurs probably used lots of signals to give different messages to each other. The signals could say "Keep away! I'm dangerous." Or "Run! An enemy is nearby!" Or "I'm big and strong. Would you like to mate with me?"

What sounds did dinosaurs make?

Like living reptiles, most dinosaurs could probably hiss or grunt. Large ones may have roared. Some, such as hadrosaurs, probably made lots of different sounds. Many hadrosaurs had strange bony crests or horns on their heads. The hadrosaur called *Parasaurolophus* (parra-saw-ro-lo-fus) had a hollow bony pipe on top of its head. The pipe was connected to air tubes in its nose and throat. Experts think it could make sounds as it breathed in and out. Perhaps it kept in touch with its herd by honking and hooting to them.

Could dinosaurs change color?

Some living reptiles, such as chameleons, can change the color of their skin. No one knows if dinosaurs could do the same or even if they were colored at all. Some horn-faced dinosaurs, such as *Chasmosaurus* (kaz-mo-saw-rus), had a large neck frill. Perhaps this frill was brightly colored. The dinosaur may have shaken its head to send messages to other *Chasmosaurus* or to scare away enemies.

Did dinosaurs have tongues?

There are no fossils of tongues, but experts know dinosaurs had tongues from fossil bones. Perhaps, like lizards today, *Struthiomimus* (stroo-thee-oh-my-mus) smelled the air with its tongue.

Maybe plant-eaters, like *Iguanodon* (ig-wa-no-don), had long, muscular tongues, like today's giraffe. These would have been great for pulling shoots and leaves off plants.

10

Could dinosaurs hear well?

Dinosaurs had ear holes like today's lizards and birds. They could probably hear, which helped them find prey and avoid danger. The hadrosaur *Corythosaurus* (co-rith-oh-saw-rus) had a hollow, bony plate on its head. It may have blown through it to trumpet warnings to the herd.

Did dinosaurs have a good sense of smell?

Most dinosaurs had well-developed nostrils. A good sense of smell would have helped them to find their food and smell friends or enemies. *Edmontosaurus* (ed-mont-oh-saw-rus) may have used a large flap of skin on top of its nose to make a noise. Perhaps it blew this up like a balloon to give a sound and make a color signal.

Did dinosaurs display like birds?

Many dinosaurs had head crests, spines or neck ruffs. Perhaps these were displayed to attract females or warn rivals. *Psittacosaurus* (si-tak-oh-saw-rus) had a beaklike mouth, just like a puffin. Perhaps its beak was brightly colored and other dinosaurs in its group could recognize it by its striped nose.

Did dinosaurs fight?

Yes, some dinosaurs sent messages by fighting. *Pachycephalosaurus* (pak-ee-sef-a-lo-saw-rus) had a thick bony skull. Its dome-shaped head looked like a crash helmet. Perhaps male *Pachycephalosaurus* had noisy head-butting contests, like today's goats. The winner may have become leader of the herd. Or perhaps they fought over female dinosaurs.

Meat-eating dinosaurs, like *Ceratosaurus* (serra-toh-saw-rus), may have had rough tongues like cats today. The rough surface would have helped scrape the last scraps of meat from bones.

Penguins need to catch slippery fish. They have small spines on their tongues to help them do this. Perhaps fish-eaters, like *Baryonyx* (bar-ee-on-ix), had spiny tongues to help them, too.

Plant-eaters

Most dinosaurs had a tasty meal within easy reach—plants. We call plant-eating animals herbivores. Herbivorous dinosaurs came in all shapes and sizes, and they fed on different kinds of plants. The shape of a dinosaur's teeth and jaws are clues to what plants it ate. Some dinosaur fossils even have the remains of their last meal in their stomachs. Conifers were the most common trees at the time of the dinosaurs. Conifer needles are tough and do not contain a lot of goodness. So many herbivores spent nearly all day eating.

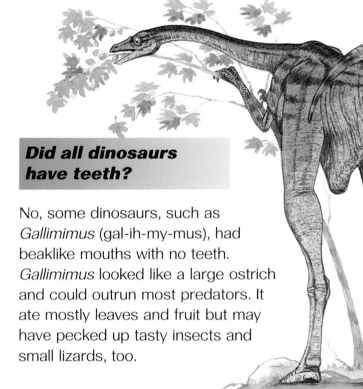

Did all dinosaurs have teeth?

No, some dinosaurs, such as *Gallimimus* (gal-ih-my-mus), had beaklike mouths with no teeth. *Gallimimus* looked like a large ostrich and could outrun most predators. It ate mostly leaves and fruit but may have pecked up tasty insects and small lizards, too.

Could dinosaurs climb trees?

Some small dinosaurs may have climbed trees in search of food. Larger ones could not climb trees. Instead, they may have reared up on their hind legs to reach as high as possible. *Plateosaurus* (plat-ee-oh-saw-rus) was one of the first big dinosaurs. It could not chew but its small, bladelike teeth were great for biting and slicing up leaves.

Were all dinosaur teeth the same?

Dinosaur teeth were all different shapes and sizes. *Iguanodon* (ig-wa-no-don) had several rows of sharp leaf-shaped teeth, which were perfect for chewing and chopping plants.

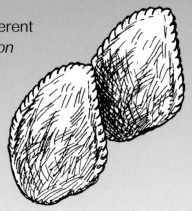

Diplodocus (dip-lo-doh-cus) could not chew. Instead, this dinosaur's teeth were peg-shaped to help it strip the leaves from branches of trees. It then swallowed the leaves whole.

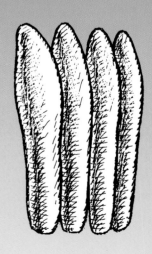

Which dinosaurs had the most teeth?

Duck-billed dinosaurs, such as *Kritosaurus* (cry-toh-saw-rus), had hundreds of teeth. These teeth were broad and flat with sharp edges and ridges—great for grinding up plants. *Kritosaurus* could probably chew up almost anything, even hard roots and woody stems.

Why did dinosaurs swallow stones?

Many plant-eating dinosaurs, such as *Mamenchisaurus* (ma-men-chee-saw-rus), could not chew. This dinosaur raked the leaves off trees with its strong, small teeth, and swallowed them whole. So, like many dinosaurs, *Mamenchisaurus* swallowed stones to help break up the food in its gut. The stones acted like a grinding mill. They moved around in its stomach, mashing up its leafy meal into a pulp.

Triceratops (try-serra-tops) had hundreds of sharp teeth. When it closed its mouth, the upper and lower teeth moved like garden shears, slicing its plant food into tiny pieces.

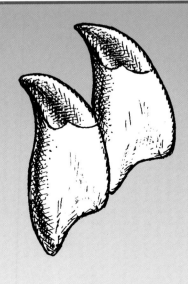

Meat-eating dinosaurs had very different teeth from plant-eaters. *Megalosaurus's* (meg-a-lo-saw-rus) huge, pointed, razor-sharp teeth curved backward to help it hold onto prey.

13

Hunters

Many dinosaurs were carnivores. They hunted, killed, and ate other animals. Like carnivores today, meat-eating dinosaurs caught their prey in different ways. Some were fierce hunters, chasing after their victims. Others hid in the undergrowth, waiting to leap out on their prey. Some dinosaurs hunted alone. Others formed savage packs. Some meat-eating dinosaurs were scavengers, feeding on dead or dying animals.

Which dinosaurs hunted in packs?

Some of the smaller dinosaurs, such as *Velociraptor* (vel-o-si-rap-tor), may have hunted in packs. This would have helped them to attack much larger animals. *Velociraptor* had sharp teeth and huge claws for tearing and slashing flesh. Even a large dinosaur could have been killed by a pack of these fierce predators.

What is a food chain?

A food chain is a list of which animals eat what. 70 million years ago it may have been like this:
1. Plants, at the start of the food chain, make their food using sunlight.

2. Plant-eating *Thescelosaurus* (thess-kel-oh-saw-rus) fed on fruits, berries, and flowering plants.

Which were the biggest meat-eaters?

The biggest meat-eating dinosaurs were the carnosaurs. They all walked on their strong hind legs and had huge heads and tiny arms. At 40 feet long, *Tarbosaurus* (tar-bo-saw-rus) was one of the largest carnosaurs. Each razor-sharp tooth was bigger than your hand. *Tarbosaurus* could move fast and may have sprinted after its prey.

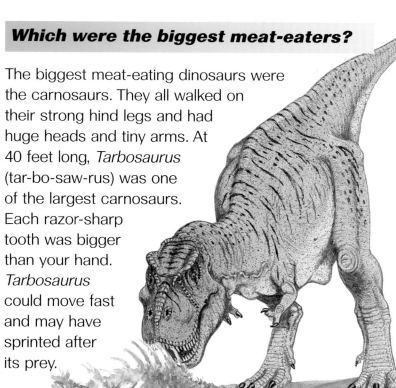

Were dinosaur hunters fast runners?

Many of the smaller meat-eating dinosaurs were very fast movers. *Dilophosaurus* (dy-lo-fo-saw-rus) may have been able to run twice as fast as you! This long-legged hunter was armed with thin, daggerlike teeth. These were great for jabbing and killing small prey and for tearing off lumps of meat.

Did dinosaurs eat fish?

Many dinosaurs lived near water, so it is possible that some ate fish. Experts think *Baryonyx* (bar-ee-on-ix) fished for its supper. Maybe it waded through the water, hooking out fish with its big claws like bears do today. *Baryonyx's* long, narrow jaws were full of small sharp teeth. Perhaps, like a crocodile, it used them to hold slippery fish before swallowing them whole.

3. *Dromaeosaurus* (dro-mee-oh-saw-rus) was a fast-moving carnivore. It fed on plant-eaters such as *Thescelosaurus*.

4. *Tyrannosaurus rex* (ty-ran-oh-saw-rus reks) was at the top of the chain. This fierce hunter preyed on plant-eaters and other meat-eaters.

15

Skin and Bone

The soft parts of an animal, like the skin, usually rot away. But a few pieces of fossil dinosaur skin have been found. Scales on their skin were hard enough to be preserved and turned to stone. This showed that, like living reptiles, some dinosaurs had scaly skins. Scales are made from a tough material called keratin. Scales gave the dinosaur's skin its colors and patterns. They also protected the dinosaur's body. Some dinosaurs had skin covered with bony lumps and bumps for extra protection.

Why did dinosaurs have plates and spines?

Some dinosaurs' bodies were covered with bony plates or spines to protect them. *Stegosaurus* (steg-oh-saw-rus) was the size of a large elephant. This plant-eating dinosaur was protected from attack by huge bony plates along its back. It also had four sharp spines on its tail. Some experts think its bony plates also helped *Stegosaurus* warm up in the sun or cool down in the shade.

Did dinosaurs wear armor?

Some plant-eating dinosaurs were protected by armorlike skin. *Saltasaurus* (salt-a-saw-rus) was the first plant-eating giant known to have armor. The skin along its back and sides was packed with pea-size lumps of bone. Its back was also studded with hunks of bone as big as your hand.

Did they have feathers?

Not all experts believe dinosaurs had feathers. But most agree that birds have evolved from a group of meat-eating dinosaurs like *Velociraptor* (vel-o-si-rap-tor).

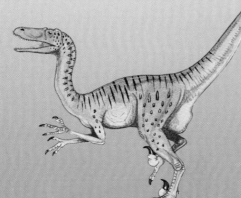

The first known bird was *Archaeopteryx* (ar-kee-op-ter-ix). It had a long bony tail, three clawed fingers, on each hand, and teeth in its beak.

Did dinosaurs have different kinds of scales?

Yes, the size and shape of dinosaurs' scales varied. Some scales were joined by bendy skin to allow dinosaurs to move. Body parts that had to bend a lot had smaller scales. *Carnotaurus* (car-noh-taw-rus) was a fierce carnivore. Its fossilized skin showed that it had rows of large, raised, coin-shaped scales along its body. It also had bony horns and rows of big, raised scales on its snout and around its eyes.

What were bone-heads?

"Bone-headed" dinosaurs had thick, bony plates on the tops of their heads. *Stygimoloch* (stij-ee-mol-ok), the "thorny devil," had rows of horns around its bony skull cap. Perhaps, like some wild goats today, *Stygimoloch* head-butted its rivals or enemies. Its bony headgear would have protected its brain from harm.

Why did some dinosaurs have a sail?

No one is sure why some dinosaurs, such as *Spinosaurus* (spy-no-saw-rus), had "sails" along their backs. *Spinosaurus*'s sail was a flap of skin held up by rods of bone which stuck up from its spine. Maybe it used its sail to attract females or threaten other males. Or perhaps the sail acted as a heating and cooling system. To warm up, the dinosaur turned the flat of its sail toward the sun.

The diving bird *Hesperornis* (hes-per-or-nis) lived at the end of the Age of Dinosaurs. It looked more like a bird of today, but it still had a bony tail and teeth in its beak.

Birds today, like the pigeon, do not have teeth, clawed wing fingers, or long bony tails. The small tail stumps hold the tail feathers.

17

Little and Large

Dinosaurs lived on Earth for 160 million years. During that time many different types of dinosaurs lived and died out. They came in all shapes and sizes. Some dinosaurs were huge. Others were the size of large lizards today. The largest dinosaurs were the plant-eating sauropods. Some of them were as tall as a four-story building. Dinosaurs were the biggest land animals that have ever lived on Earth. No really tiny dinosaurs have been found.

Were all dinosaurs giants?

No, many dinosaurs were quite small. *Saltopus* (salt-oh-pus), one of the smallest found, was about the size of a chicken. This speedy hunter was so quick it could catch flying insects and fast-moving lizards. *Saltopus*'s small size meant that it could hide from its enemies easily. Also, being small meant it needed less food than bigger dinosaurs.

Were dinosaurs as tall as trees?

Sauropods had huge barrel-shaped bodies, short legs, whiplike tails, and long necks. If they reared up, their long necks could reach to over 65 feet. They would have towered over many trees. The longest dinosaur may have been *Seismosaurus* (size-mo-saw-rus). An adult was over 130 feet long—about 10 family cars lined up nose to tail.

How do scientists weigh dinosaurs?

No one can weigh a real dinosaur, but scientists can get an idea using a model.

1. First, they make an accurate scale model of the dinosaur.

2. The model is placed in a container full of water. Some of the water will overflow into the outside container. This water is collected.

Which dinosaur had the biggest head?

Torosaurus (tor-oh-saw-rus) had the biggest head of any known dinosaur. This large plant-eater was as long as an elephant and weighed as much as five rhinoceroses. Its huge skull bones and the large frill over its neck were the size of a big dining-room table!

What did small dinosaurs eat?

Some small dinosaurs ate plants while others hunted insects, tiny reptiles, or other small animals. *Microceratops* (my-cro-serra-tops) was about as big as a large pet cat. This tiny plant-eater probably nipped off juicy shoots with its horny beak. Then it sliced them up with its scissorlike back teeth.

Which was the biggest meat-eater?

The famous *Tyrannosaurus rex* (ty-ran-oh-saw-rus reks) was one of the biggest meat-eating dinosaurs. It was over 40 feet long and three times as tall as a man. Its huge jaws were big enough to swallow a person whole and its razor-sharp teeth were as long as a human hand.

3. The water collected takes up the same amount of space as the model dinosaur. This amount is called the volume. From this, scientists can work out the volume of the actual dinosaur.

4. Scientists know how to work out the weight of a modern reptile, such as an alligator, from its volume of water. They use the same method to estimate how much dinosaurs weighed, too.

Dinosaur Weapons

From fossil remains we can tell that many dinosaurs were armed with deadly weapons. They used these to attack each other or to defend themselves. A dinosaur's weapons were parts of its body—its teeth, horns, claws, or tail. Meat-eating dinosaurs were built to kill. They attacked their victims with sharp teeth and slashing claws. Some plant-eating dinosaurs had weapons to defend themselves against these hunters or perhaps to fight rival males. They used sharp horns, clublike tails, or armor plating to defeat their attackers.

Did dinosaurs have horns?

Some plant-eating dinosaurs, called ceratopians, developed huge horns. They may have charged at their enemies, like a rhinoceros does today. *Pentaceratops* (pen-ta-serra-tops) had a huge horned frill and three horns. It was about 23 feet long and weighed three times as much as a rhinoceros. Most of the time it grazed peacefully on plants.

Which dinosaur had a club?

The armored dinosaur *Euoplocephalus* (you-oh-plo-sef-al-us) had a deadly club on its tail. This well-defended plant-eater was as long as an elephant and heavier than a rhinoceros. Its tail ended in two heavy lumps of bone. If attacked, *Euoplocephalus* may have turned around and swiped its enemy with its heavy tail-club.

How do scientists reconstruct dinosaurs?

When fossils are first dug up, they are just a jumble of bones. Horns, claws, and neck and tail bones are mixed up with ribs and leg bones. Often there are bones missing.

1. Scientists lay out the bones in their correct order. If a bone is missing, the scientists make a replacement from a tough material called fiberglass.

Could dinosaurs kill with their claws?

Many dinosaurs had claws. *Deinonychus* (dy-non-i-kus) had very large, killing claws. The second toe of each back foot was armed with a deadly, 4¾-inch-long claw. This small, swift hunter probably ran and leaped on its victim.

Why did Diplodocus have thumb spikes?

No one knows for sure, but it may have used them as weapons. *Diplodocus* (dip-lo-doh-cus) was huge. It was as heavy as two elephants and as long as a tennis court. Few predators would attack such a large beast. But, if a carnosaur like *Allosaurus* (al-oh-saw-rus) did attack, *Diplodocus* fought back. It probably lashed its enemy with its tail and jabbed it with its thumb spikes.

Which dinosaur wore spikes and shields?

Some armored dinosaurs, such as *Edmontonia* (ed-mon-toh-nee-ah), were built like tanks. Its body was covered with thick, bony shields. Sharp spikes on its shoulders and down the sides of its body gave greater protection. The only place a predator could hurt this dinosaur was in its soft underbelly.

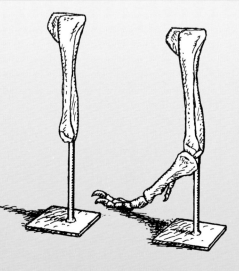

2. An engineer makes a steel frame, called an armature. The leg bones are then rested on the armature. The rest of the bones are slowly added to build the dinosaur.

3. The tail and skull are added last, completing the dinosaur skeleton. Bones can also be hung from a ceiling by steel wires instead of being rested on a support.

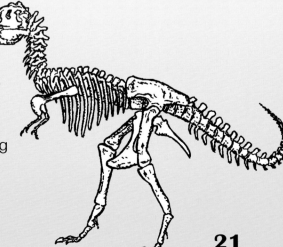

Fast and Slow

Just like animals today, dinosaurs moved at different speeds. Some could run fast. Others lumbered along slowly. Their shape, size, and the speed at which they moved depended on how they lived. Most hunters had to be fast to chase after their prey. Some of the smaller meat-eating dinosaurs could run as fast as a race horse. Giant, plant-eating sauropods walked slowly. They were too heavy to run. Medium-size herbivores may have trotted quickly like today's rhinoceroses. Small plant-eaters had to be quick to outrun their enemies.

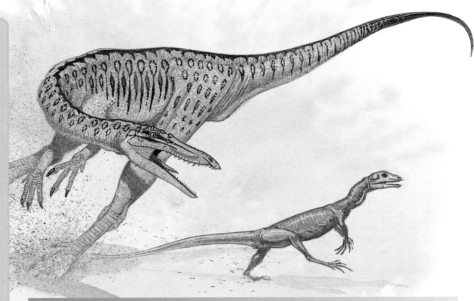

Why did some dinosaurs walk on two legs?

Walking on two legs helps an animal to move more quickly. *Coelophysis* (see-loh-fy-sis) was a slim, light dinosaur. It was 10 feet long and stood about as tall as a person. But it only weighed about 55 pounds—about as much as a 7-year-old child. It had powerful back legs and could probably turn at speed to race after its prey.

How fast could dinosaurs run?

No one is sure how fast dinosaurs could run. Experts study a dinosaur's footprints to try to work out its speed. They also look at the way it is built and compare it with animals today. *Struthiomimus* (stroo-thee-oh-my-mus) had long, strong back legs like an ostrich. It may have sped along at up to 50 miles an hour.

How do we measure dinosaur speed?

Speed can be calculated by the distance between footprints and foot size. The deep prints of sauropods, like *Brachiosaurus,* are close together, showing they plodded along.

These footprints are quite close together. They were probably made by a walking *Iguanodon* (ig-wa-no-don). *Iguanodon* had big back feet and smaller front feet. They could walk on all fours or on two legs.

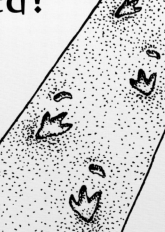

Which were the slowest dinosaurs?

The armored dinosaurs were among the slowest movers. But this did not matter as they were well protected from attack. *Ankylosaurus* (an-ky-lo-saw-rus) was one of largest of the armored dinosaurs. It was longer than a big bus and covered with heavy, bony plates. Its tail ended in a huge bony club the size of a large suitcase.

Could huge plant-eaters run?

Most huge plant-eaters were too heavy to run. *Brachiosaurus* (bra-kee-oh-saw-rus) was one of the biggest dinosaurs. It was over 82 feet long and up to 60 feet tall. It weighed over 66 tons. That's more than 12 elephants! It needed huge legs like pillars to support it. *Brachiosaurus* probably plodded along like an elephant. If it had tried to run, the shock would have broken its legs.

Did big meat-eaters move fast?

Many large carnosaurs could probably run fast over short distances. *Ceratosaurus* (serra-a-toh-saw-rus) was 20 feet long, twice the height of a man, and weighed as much as a hippopotamus. But it could probably run much faster than a hippo. *Ceratosaurus*'s body was built for speed. It had long, strong back legs, a slim head, and a long tail to help it balance. It probably dashed after its prey over short distances, like lions do today.

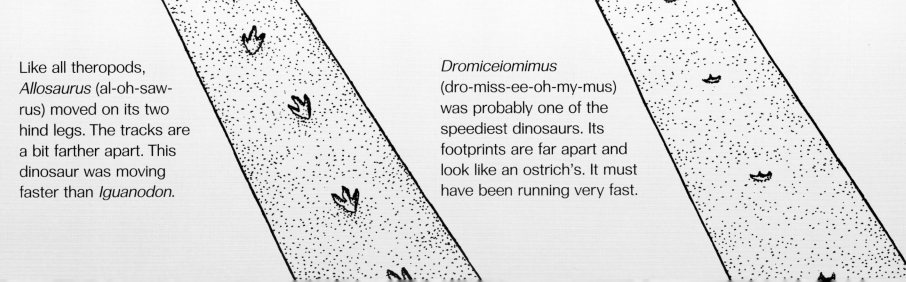

Like all theropods, *Allosaurus* (al-oh-saw-rus) moved on its two hind legs. The tracks are a bit farther apart. This dinosaur was moving faster than *Iguanodon*.

Dromiceiomimus (dro-miss-ee-oh-my-mus) was probably one of the speediest dinosaurs. Its footprints are far apart and look like an ostrich's. It must have been running very fast.

Sea Reptiles

Although some dinosaurs could probably swim, none lived in the water all of the time. While dinosaurs ruled the land, other giant reptiles ruled the prehistoric oceans. Mosasaurs, plesiosaurs, and pliosaurs were fierce hunters. They had long jaws full of sharp teeth to snap up fish and other sea creatures. Giant crocodiles and turtles also roamed the ancient seas.

How big were sea reptiles?

The largest sea reptiles were the plesiosaurs (ple-zee-oh-sors) and pliosaurs (ply-oh-sors). Plesiosaurs, like the one shown here, had fat bodies, long necks, and short tails. The biggest grew to about 50 feet long. They used their paddle-shaped legs to power them through the water. The pliosaur *Kronosaurus* (kroh-no-saw-rus) was 56 feet long with a head the size of a car!

What did sea reptiles eat?

Most sea reptiles fed on fish, squid, and shellfish called ammonites. Mosasaurs (mo-za-sors) were fast-swimming hunters. They snapped up other sea creatures in their huge mouths, filled with rows of sharp teeth. Mosasaurs grew to about 40 feet long. They were the largest ever lizards and are related to today's monitor lizards.

Are prehistoric reptiles alive today?

Yes, turtles and crocodiles still exist although their prehistoric forms were much bigger. *Deinosuchus* (die-no-sook-us) was a huge 53-foot-long crocodile.

Deinosuchus's largest living relative, the saltwater crocodile, is about 23 feet long. It lives along the coasts of Australia and Southeast Asia.

Did sea reptiles lay eggs?

Most sea reptiles came ashore to lay their eggs like turtles do today. But ichthyosaurs (ik-thee-oh-sors) gave birth to live young, like today's dolphins. The smooth shape of an ichthyosaur was ideal for speeding through water. Its strong tail powered it along and its paddlelike legs were great for steering. Like all sea reptiles, ichthyosaurs had to come to the surface of the sea to breathe.

Did dinosaurs live by the sea?

Several dinosaurs, like the meat-eating *Megalosaurus* (meg-a-lo-saw-rus), probably lived near the water. This big carnivore may have prowled along the beach on the lookout for prey. Perhaps it combed the sand searching for dead animals.

Could dinosaurs swim?

No one knows for sure but, like most animals today, dinosaurs could probably swim if they had to. *Cetiosaurus* (see-tee-oh-saw-rus) may have paddled as it searched for food. But it would not have spent much time in the sea. The salt in the water could have damaged its scales and skin.

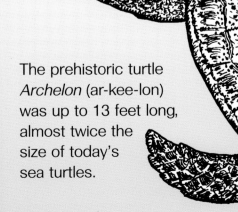

The prehistoric turtle *Archelon* (ar-kee-lon) was up to 13 feet long, almost twice the size of today's sea turtles.

Archelon's largest living relative, the leatherback turtle, is about 8 feet long. The leatherback roams the world's oceans, feeding on jellyfish.

25

Death of the Dinosaurs

Dinosaurs lived on Earth for over 160 million years. They first appeared about 230 million years ago. The last dinosaurs roamed the world 65 million years ago. Then all dinosaurs died out— they became extinct. Experts believe that they disappeared gradually in some areas and more suddenly in others. Dinosaurs were not the only living things to disappear. Many other animals and plants died out at the same time. The reasons for this mass extinction are not known. Scientists have come up with many theories.

Did dinosaurs freeze to death?

Triceratops (try-serra-tops) lived at the end of the Age of Dinosaurs. The climate began to change at about this time. The tropical climate of North America became cooler and more seasonal. Perhaps some dinosaurs could not adapt to these changes and could not stand up to the cold. There have been many mass extinctions during the life of Earth. No one is sure why they occur.

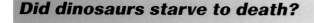

Did dinosaurs starve to death?

Albertosaurus (al-ber-toh-saw-rus) was one of the last dinosaurs to survive. This large carnosaur was similar to *Tyrannosaurus rex* (ty-ran-oh-saw-rus reks). Did these huge creatures die out from lack of suitable food? Or did they die from disease? Their death may have been caused by more than one thing. Perhaps we shall never know.

When did the dinosaurs live?

Dinosaurs appeared during the Triassic. *Eoraptor* (ee-oh-rap-tor) is the earliest known carnivore.

Dinosaurs, such as the plant-eating *Diplodocus* (dip-lo-doh-cus), appeared in the Jurassic.

Mesozoic Era—The Age of Dinosaurs

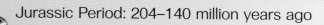

Triassic Period: 245–204 million years ago

Jurassic Period: 204–140 million years ago

What do scientists think happened?

Most scientists think that the most likely cause for the death of the dinosaurs was a gigantic rock from space. They have found traces of a huge crater off the coast of Mexico. They think it was caused by a huge chunk of rock, or meteorite, about 6 miles across, hitting the earth. This would have thrown up masses of dust and ash. The dust would have formed a huge cloud, blocking out the Sun's light and heat. Plants and animals that could not cope with these conditions would have died out.

Tyrannosaurus rex was one of the last dinosaurs to develop in the Cretaceous Period.

With the dinosaurs extinct, the Age of Mammals began with mammals like *Taeniolabis* (ty-nee-oh-lah-bis).

Cenozoic Era—The Age of Mammals

Cretaceous Period: 140–65 million years ago

Tertiary Period: 65–2 million years ago

What do you know about dinosaurs?

1 **What size was Oviraptor?**
a) The size of an elephant
b) The size of a wolf
c) The size of a mouse

2 **Why did some plant-eating dinosaurs live in herds?**
a) Because they liked company
b) For safety and protection
c) To help build larger nests

3 **When were the first dinosaur eggs found?**
a) In 1922
b) In 1822
c) In 1992

4 **Which of these dinosaurs was a hunter?**
a) *Deinonychus*
b) *Iguanodon*
c) *Diplodocus*

5 **Which parts of the body are most likely to fossilize?**
a) Blood
b) Muscles
c) Bones

6 **Which of these dinosaurs had peg-shaped teeth?**
a) *Gallimimus*
b) *Diplodocus*
c) *Triceratops*

7 **What were the giant plant-eating dinosaurs called?**
a) Sauropods
b) Carnosaurs
c) Ornithopods

8 **Which of these prehistoric animals lived in the sea?**
a) Stegosaurs
b) Ichthyosaurs
c) Hadrosaurs

9 **Which of these dinosaurs was the fastest?**
a) *Allosaurus*
b) *Ankylosaurus*
c) *Dromiceiomimus*

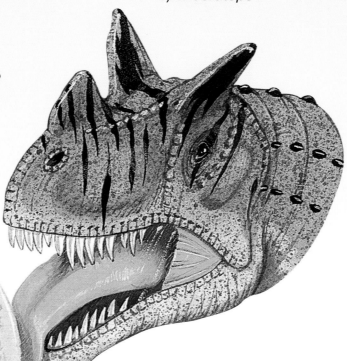

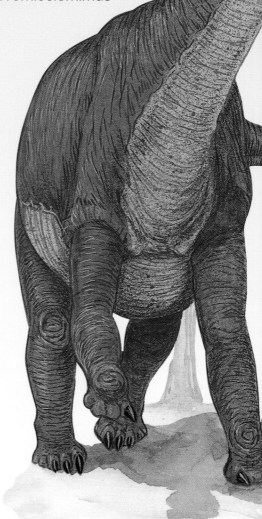

10 How long was Tyrannosaurus rex?
a) Over 40 inches long
b) Over 40 feet long
c) Over 40 miles long

11 What is the correct name for The Age of Dinosaurs?
a) The Mesozoic Era
b) The Cenozoic Era
c) The Prehistoric Era

12 When did dinosaurs become extinct?
a) 245 million years ago
b) 160 million years ago
c) 65 million years ago

13 Which of these dinosaurs had no teeth?
a) Megalosaurus
b) Triceratops
c) Gallimimus

14 Which reptiles today are related to ancient Deinosuchus?
a) Turtles
b) Monitor lizards
c) Saltwater crocodiles

15 Which dinosaur had a club on its tail?
a) Pentaceratops
b) Euoplocephalus
c) Edmontonia

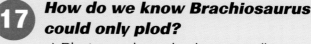

16 What is the name of the first known bird?
a) Hesperornis
b) Archaeopteryx
c) Struthiomimus

17 How do we know Brachiosaurus could only plod?
a) Photographs only show it walking
b) Its fossil footprints are deep and close together
c) Its tail was too long for it to run

18 Which of these prehistoric animals was a mammal?
a) Taeniolabis
b) Archelon
c) Maiasaura

19 When did Diplodocus first appear?
a) In the Cretaceous Period
b) In the Jurassic Period
c) In the Triassic Period

20 What is the name of a dinosaur expert?
a) A zoologist
b) A palaeontologist
c) A pharmacist

Index

Answers to Quiz

1	b) The size of a wolf	**6**	b) *Diplodocus*	**14**	c) Saltwater crocodiles
2	b) For safety and protection	**7**	a) Sauropods	**15**	b) *Euoplocephalus*
3	a) In 1922	**8**	b) Ichthyosaurs	**16**	b) *Archaeopteryx*
4	a) *Deinonychus*	**9**	c) *Dromiceiomimus*	**17**	b) Its fossil footprints are deep and close together
5	c) Bones	**10**	b) Over 40 feet long	**18**	a) *Taeniolabis*
		11	a) The Mesozoic Era	**19**	b) In the Jurassic Period
		12	c) 65 million years ago	**20**	b) A palaeontologist
		13	c) *Gallimimus*		